by Uta Haagen-Dasz

ISBN 1-56850-045-9

© 1994, Chicago Plays, Inc.

Chicago Plays
2632 N. Lincoln
Chicago, IL 60614

Foreword

> "You damn fools,
> you can take my advice
> or go to hell."
>
> -Uta Haagen-Dasz
> credo, HD Studios

Nothing impresses agents more than Karaoke experience.

Contempt for Acting Chicago Plays Inc.

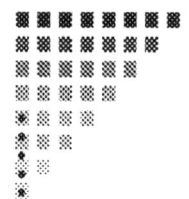

To guarantee you get the part, bring a loaded weapon.

Contempt for Acting

Chicago Plays Inc.

Perform all your monologues as if you were impersonating William Shattner.

Contempt for Acting — Chicago Plays Inc.

Don't pay royalties. Playwrights will lick your shoes to get their shows produced.

Contempt for Acting — Chicago Plays Inc.

If you're playing an alcoholic, habitually show up to rehearsals drunk.

Contempt for Acting　　　　Chicago Plays Inc.

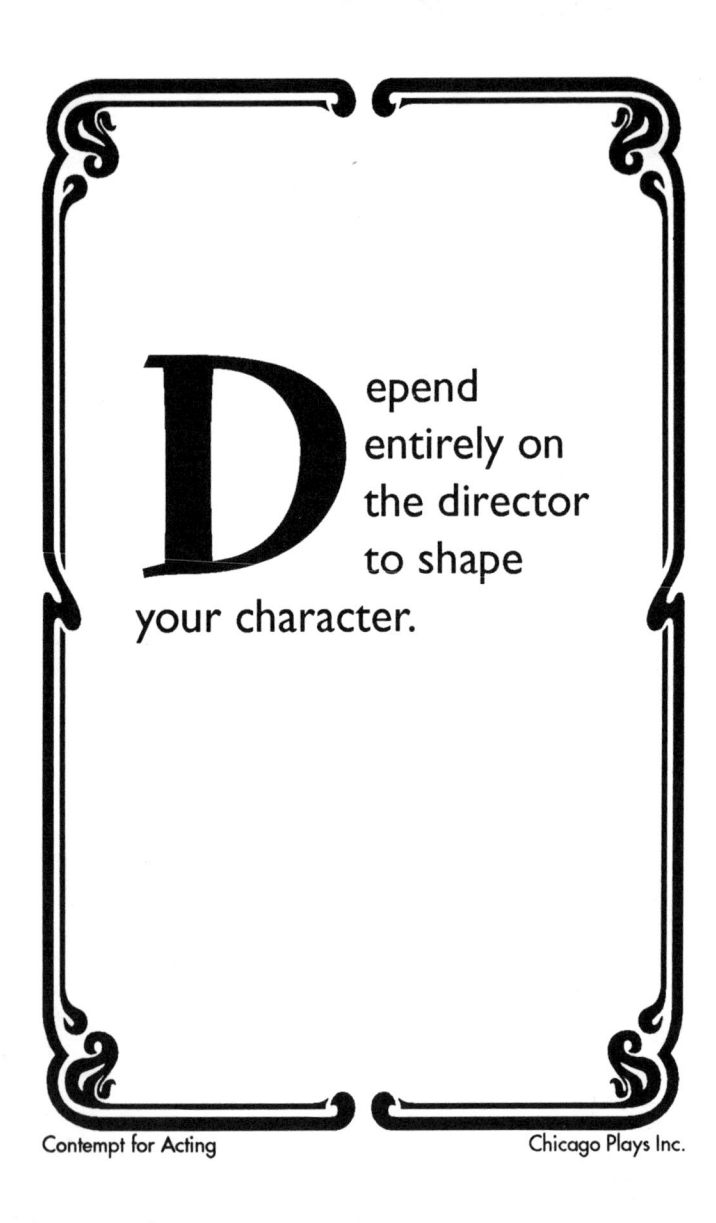

Depend entirely on the director to shape your character.

Contempt for Acting

Chicago Plays Inc.

Set a little time every day to pray to your acting coach.

Contempt for Acting

Chicago Plays Inc.

If a monologue is in more than one monologue book, then it's really good.

Contempt for Acting — Chicago Plays Inc.

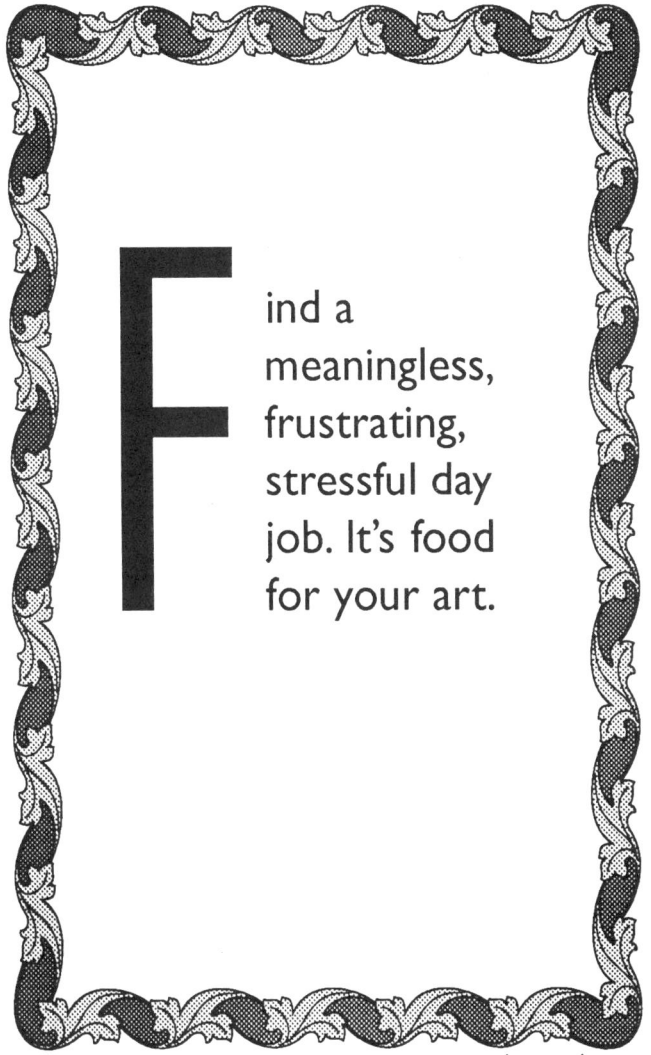

Find a meaningless, frustrating, stressful day job. It's food for your art.

Contempt for Acting   Chicago Plays Inc.

The monologue you learned in high school forensics will come in handy for the rest of your life.

Contempt for Acting Chicago Plays Inc.

The more you pay your agent, the harder she'll work for you.

Contempt for Acting   Chicago Plays Inc.

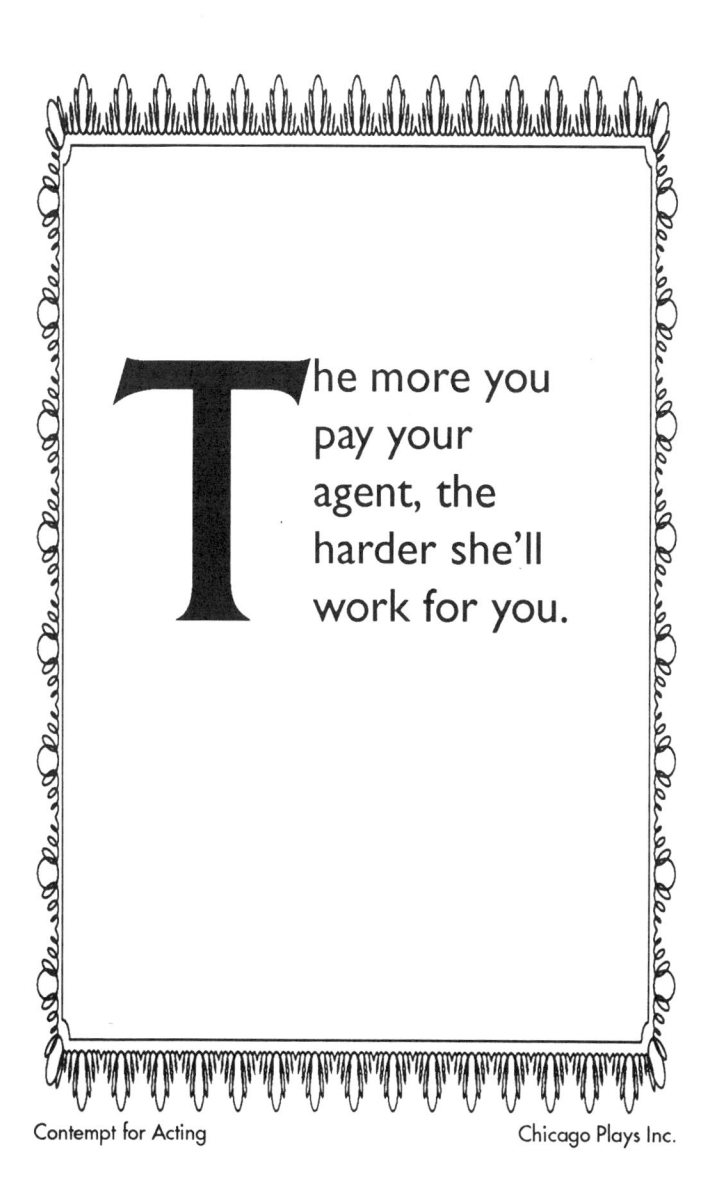

Go through life as if everyone were a casting director looking for the next Hot Young Thing.

Contempt for Acting — Chicago Plays Inc.

*O*nly read plays other people tell you are good.

Contempt for Acting — Chicago Plays Inc.

If someone says "You'll never work in this town again," believe him.

Contempt for Acting   Chicago Plays Inc.

There's no such thing as "other actors," only bitter competition trying to squash you.

Contempt for Acting   Chicago Plays Inc.

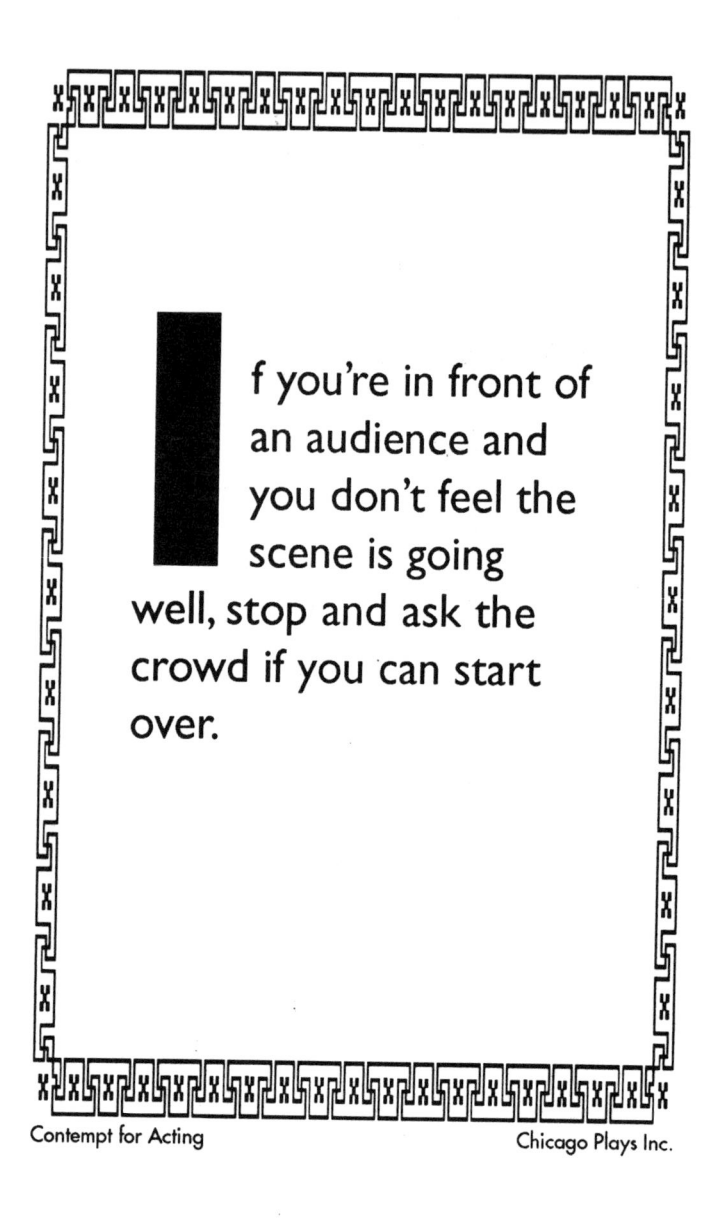

If you're in front of an audience and you don't feel the scene is going well, stop and ask the crowd if you can start over.

Contempt for Acting   Chicago Plays Inc.

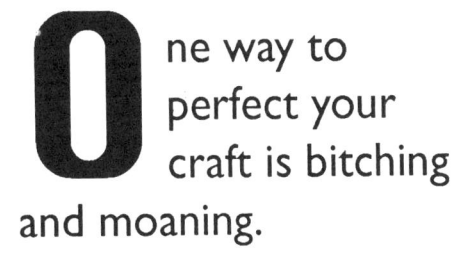

One way to perfect your craft is bitching and moaning.

Contempt for ActingChicago Plays Inc.

If you don't get the part you were born to play, sue.

Contempt for Acting Chicago Plays Inc.

*F*ame is only a two-day, $299 workshop away.

Contempt for Acting   Chicago Plays Inc.

Don't bother reading plays for monologues. Just buy one of those great monologue books.

Contempt for Acting   Chicago Plays Inc.

Researching your role is for nerds. Extensive rehearsals are for morons. You're an actor. Wing it.

Contempt for Acting — Chicago Plays Inc.

Let your costuming do your acting for you.

Contempt for Acting — Chicago Plays Inc.

Pauses and exclamation points are the bread and butter of good acting.

Being oblivious to the rest of the world is imperative to proper Method Acting.

Contempt for Acting   Chicago Plays Inc.

Always let the audience know that you're much smarter than the character you're playing.

Contempt for Acting Chicago Plays Inc.

The best way to be discovered is to do porno.

Contempt for Acting

Chicago Plays Inc.

If you're in front of an audience and you forget your lines, run like hell.

Contempt for Acting — Chicago Plays Inc.

Imagine your life as one giant soap opera.

Contempt for Acting　　　　　　　　　　　　　　　Chicago Plays Inc.

Only play parts with the same first name as you.

Contempt for Acting — Chicago Plays Inc.

No matter how demeaning, insulting, and trite the writing is, no matter how difficult the director or other actors are, no matter how unsatisfied with the character you are asked to play, never turn down a role.

Contempt for Acting — Chicago Plays Inc.

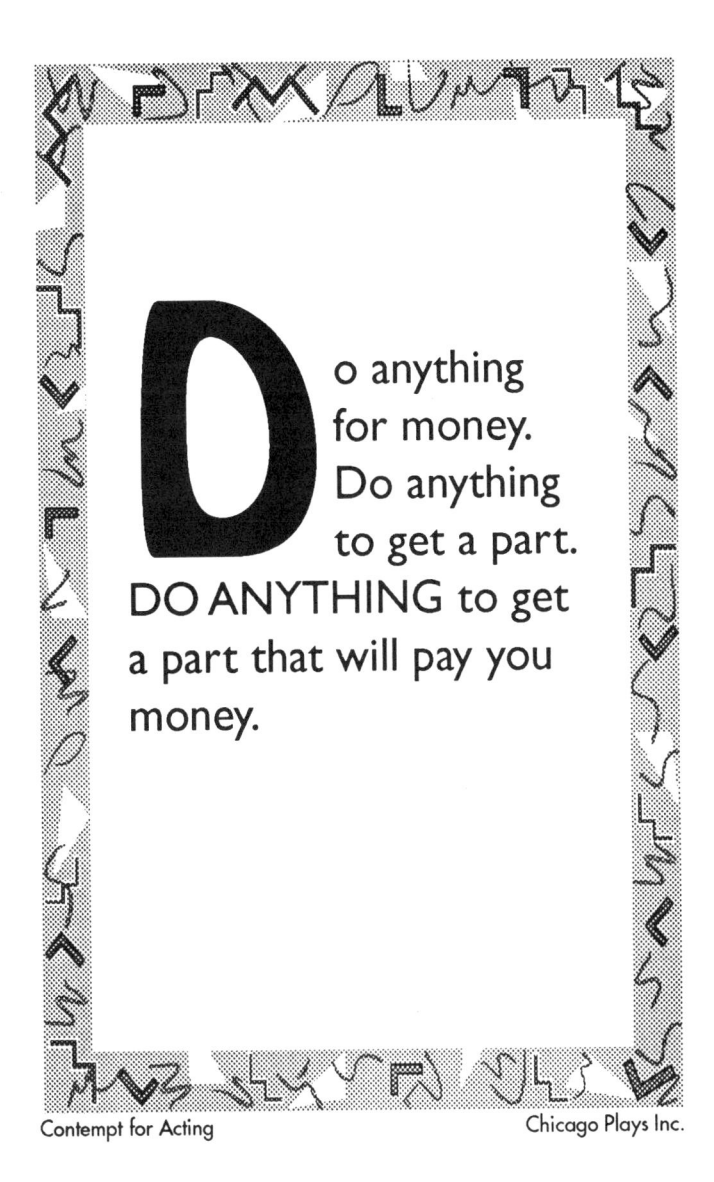

Do anything for money. Do anything to get a part. DO ANYTHING to get a part that will pay you money.

Contempt for Acting — Chicago Plays Inc.

Study today's best actors. They're often found in Calvin Klein ads.

Contempt for Acting   Chicago Plays Inc.

Plant subliminal messages by writing "SUPERSTAR" all over your resume.

Contempt for Acting

Chicago Plays Inc.

Really great actors can lose themselves and transform themselves into whoever's hot in Hollywood.

Contempt for Acting — Chicago Plays Inc.

Never play a part that involves messing up your hair.

Contempt for Acting — Chicago Plays Inc.

Anyone who's not in the Business is merely a distraction from what's important in life, and should be treated as such.

Contempt for Acting — Chicago Plays Inc.

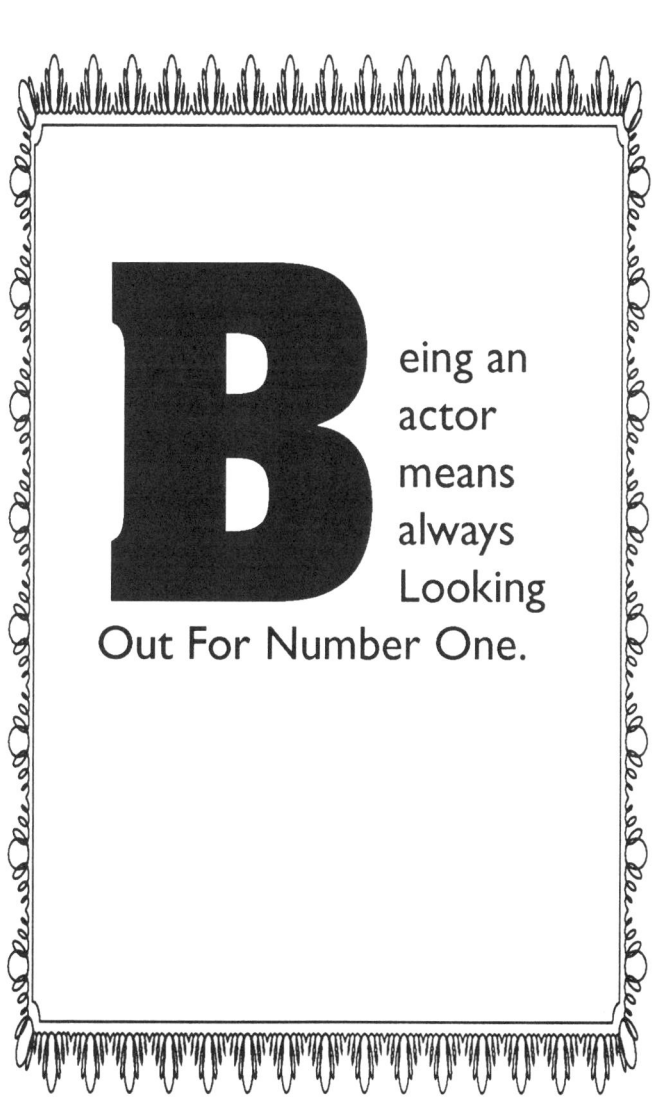

Being an actor means always Looking Out For Number One.

Contempt for Acting   Chicago Plays Inc.

Always trash the shows that didn't cast you.

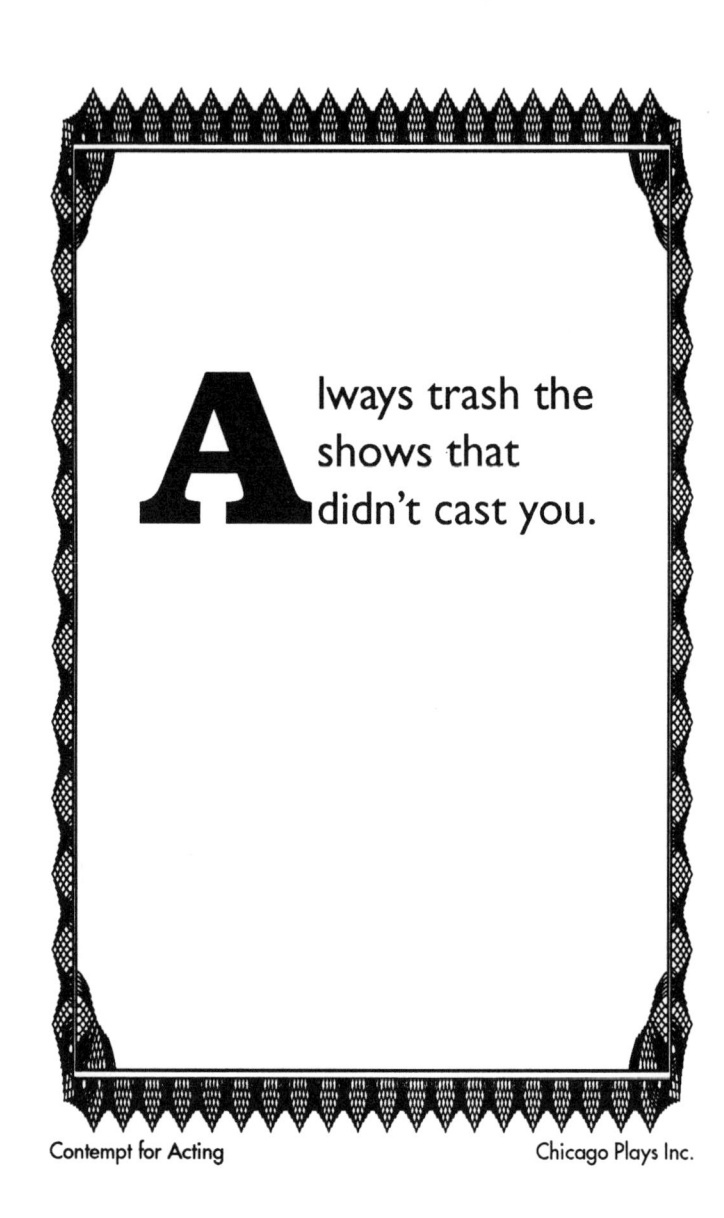

Contempt for Acting Chicago Plays Inc.

If you're not sure what you should do onstage, smoke.

Contempt for Acting — Chicago Plays Inc.

Other actors are merely the object of your putdowns.

Contempt for Acting — Chicago Plays Inc.

The only way to play a character is the way your acting coach told you.

Contempt for Acting — Chicago Plays Inc.

Always take the easy way out.

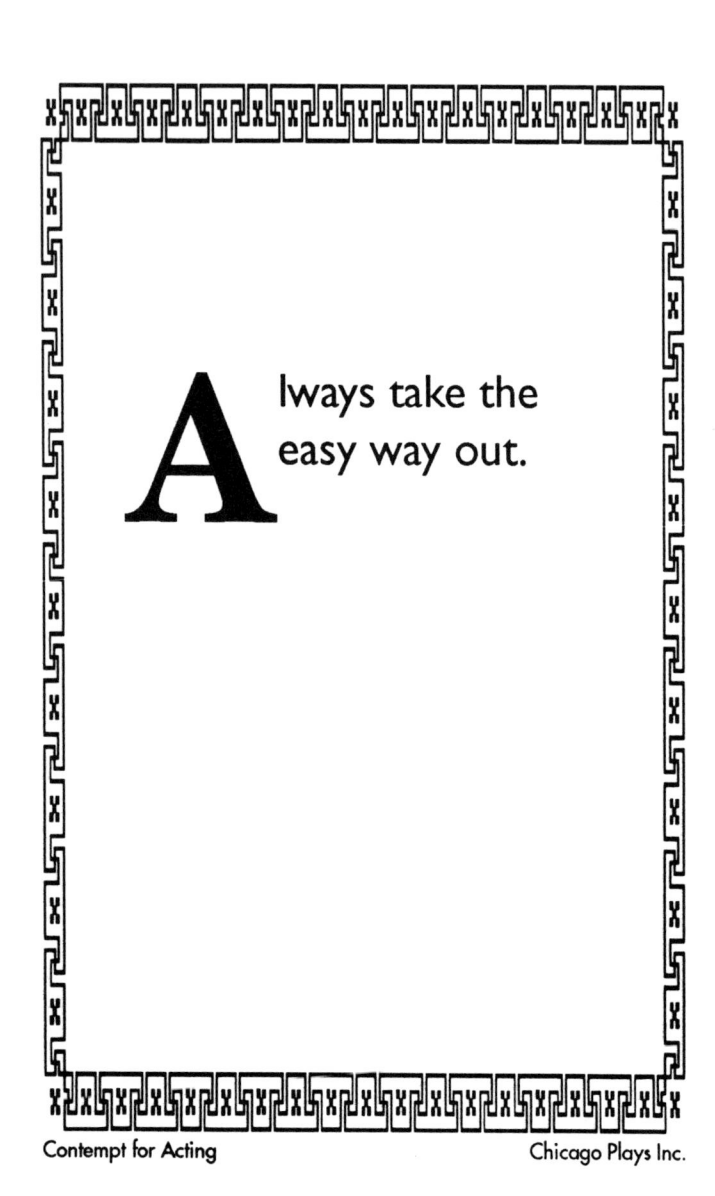

Contempt for Acting   Chicago Plays Inc.

It's not stealing if the person you stole it from isn't famous.

Contempt for Acting   Chicago Plays Inc.

Spend all your money placing photos of yourself in local rags. Use the caption, "Desperate Actor."

Contempt for Acting   Chicago Plays Inc.

*O*nce the show opens, the director can't make you stick to the blocking.

Contempt for Acting — Chicago Plays Inc.

Practice acting in commercials by endorsing your deodorant in everyday situations.

Contempt for Acting   Chicago Plays Inc.

It's useless to read the scenes in the play that don't have your character in them.

Contempt for Acting   Chicago Plays Inc.

Get all your acting wisdom from paperback books.

Contempt for Acting

Chicago Plays Inc.

Don't worry if you don't know what a word in the script means. The audience probably doesn't either.

All you need to do a Tennessee Williams play is a good Southern accent.

Contempt for Acting Chicago Plays Inc.

All you need to do a Sam Shepard play is to act crazy. Drooling is especially effective.

If you're doing a play by David Mamet, feel free to throw in some extra 'fuck's.

Contempt for Acting Chicago Plays Inc.

If you're in a Chekhov play, the best way to act is like a very sad zombie.

Contempt for Acting

Chicago Plays Inc.

For extra realism onstage, use real drugs.

Contempt for Acting — Chicago Plays Inc.

If you want to meet an agent, break into her office in the middle of the night and hide until she arrives in the morning.

Contempt for Acting Chicago Plays Inc.

Since designers can't help you advance your career, there's no need to give them the time of day.

Contempt for Acting · Chicago Plays Inc.

Really good agents hate actors.

Contempt for Acting

Chicago Plays Inc.

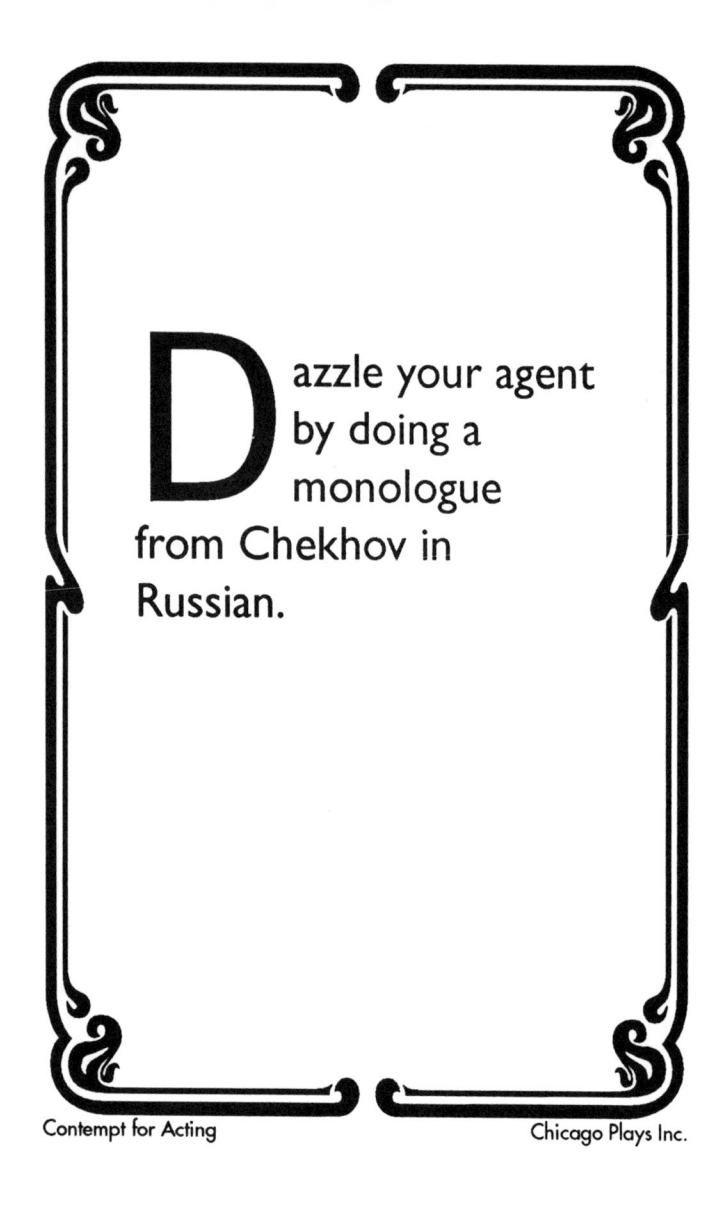

Dazzle your agent by doing a monologue from Chekhov in Russian.

Contempt for Acting

Chicago Plays Inc.

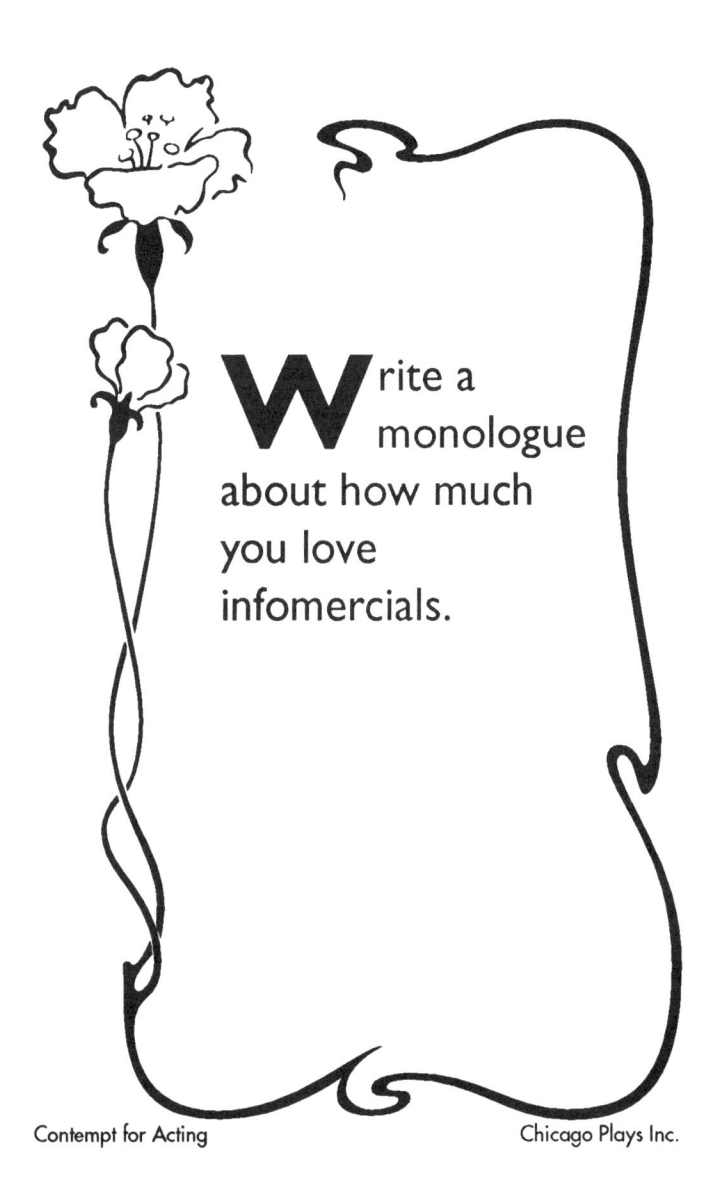

Write a monologue about how much you love infomercials.

Contempt for Acting

Chicago Plays Inc.

Calling your agent late at night often spurs extra employment.

Contempt for Acting   Chicago Plays Inc.

Name drop as often as possible.

Contempt for Acting — Chicago Plays Inc.

Don't bother learning your lines. Just find interesting props large enough to hold your script.

Contempt for Acting Chicago Plays Inc.

𝕴nvest in your future: Plastic Surgery.

Contempt for Acting					Chicago Plays Inc.

Take criticism personally.

Contempt for Acting   Chicago Plays Inc.

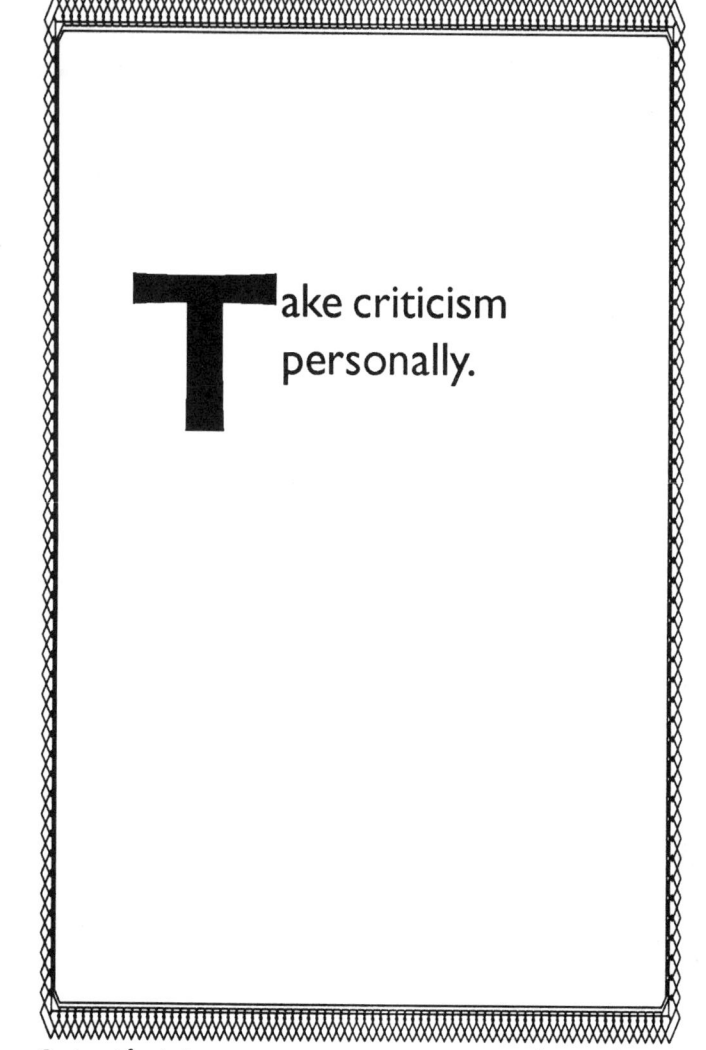

If one character has all the funny lines, take some for yourself.

Contempt for Acting — Chicago Plays Inc.

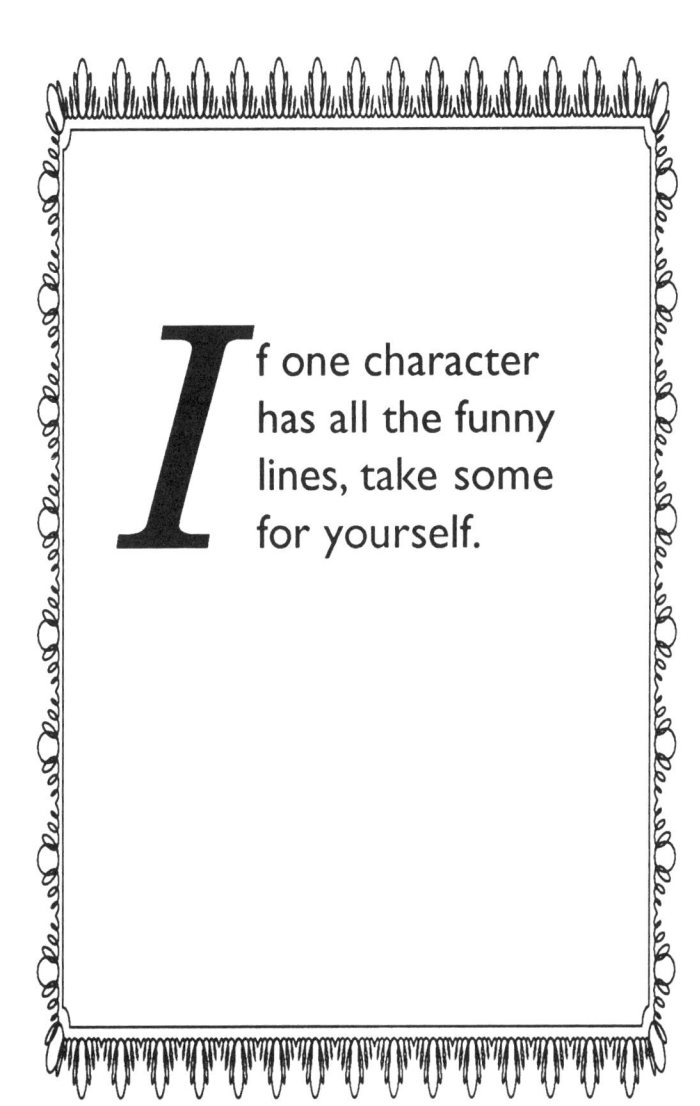

A program isn't a program unless it has at least three inside jokes.

Contempt for Acting   Chicago Plays Inc.

Treat every script as if it were an episode of **Three's Company**.

Contempt for Acting   Chicago Plays Inc.

You only live once, so do it for the money.

Contempt for Acting — Chicago Plays Inc.

Nothing makes an audition piece more authentic than chewing gum.

Contempt for Acting — Chicago Plays Inc.

Auditors love nothing more than the attentions of a flirt.

Contempt for Acting   Chicago Plays Inc.

Use the same monologue for every audition.

Contempt for Acting — Chicago Plays Inc.

Angry actors are cool. Be one.

Contempt for Acting — Chicago Plays Inc.

There's no higher compliment an actor can receive than being called the next James Dean.

Contempt for Acting Chicago Plays Inc.

Get all your aggressions out on your agent's receptionist.

Contempt for Acting　　　　　　　　　　　　Chicago Plays Inc.

Keep your networking skills strong with good gossip.

Contempt for Acting — Chicago Plays Inc.

Nothing cleanses the soul like good commercial copy.

Contempt for Acting Chicago Plays Inc.

Never sell your soul, unless it's for a really fast car.

Contempt for Acting — Chicago Plays Inc.

The most important part of your training as an actor is hair care.

Contempt for Acting   Chicago Plays Inc.

Happiness is a guest appearance on **Melrose Place**.

Contempt for Acting — Chicago Plays Inc.

L aurence Olivier may have been a great actor, but he never had the #1 TV show in America.

Contempt for Acting

Chicago Plays Inc.

If you want to make a difference, make made-for-TV movies.

Contempt for Acting   Chicago Plays Inc.

Doing Shakespeare in the Park will never help you get Discovered.

Contempt for Acting   Chicago Plays Inc.

Scruples will only get in the way of your career.

Contempt for Acting — Chicago Plays Inc.

The best place to audition is your answering machine.

Contempt for Acting   Chicago Plays Inc.

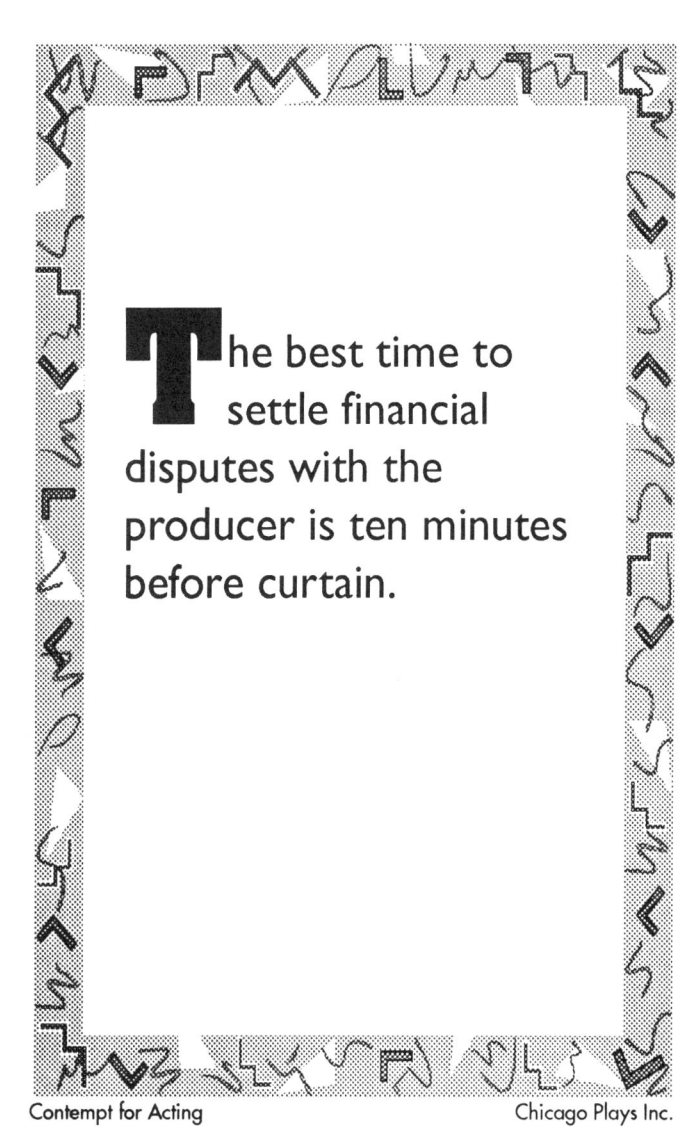

The best time to settle financial disputes with the producer is ten minutes before curtain.

Contempt for Acting   Chicago Plays Inc.

To relieve the tedium of a long run, trade parts.

Contempt for Acting

Chicago Plays Inc.

Get your monologues by memorizing speeches from your favorite soaps.

Contempt for Acting — Chicago Plays Inc.

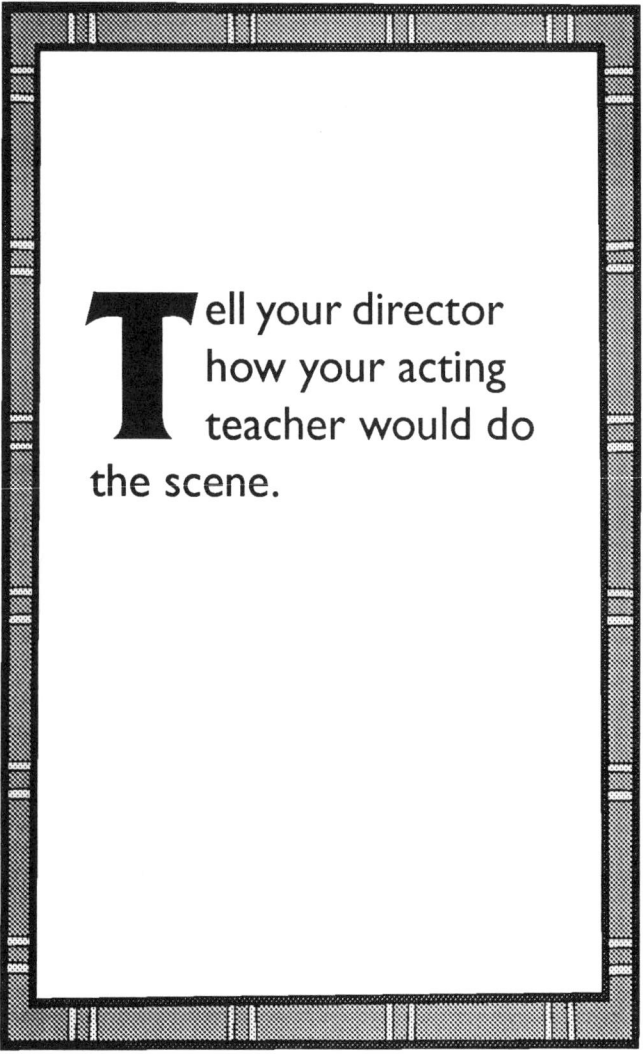

Tell your director how your acting teacher would do the scene.

Contempt for Acting — Chicago Plays Inc.

If you never show your vulnerable side, everyone will think you're cool.

Contempt for Acting   Chicago Plays Inc.

If you can't be an actor, at least dress like one.

Contempt for Acting

Chicago Plays Inc.

When interviewing an agent, break the ice by asking at what price he would sell his mother.

Contempt for Acting

Chicago Plays Inc.

If you get tired of changing into your costume, just go onstage in what you're wearing that day.

Contempt for Acting — Chicago Plays Inc.

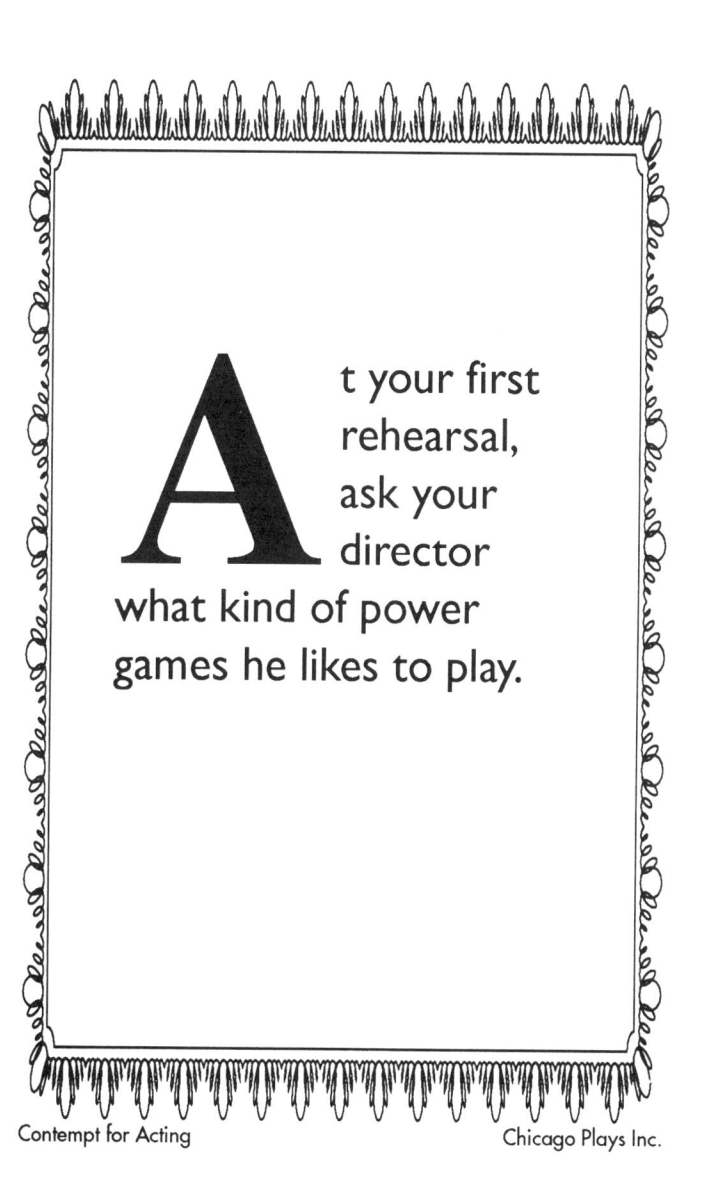

At your first rehearsal, ask your director what kind of power games he likes to play.

Contempt for Acting — Chicago Plays Inc.

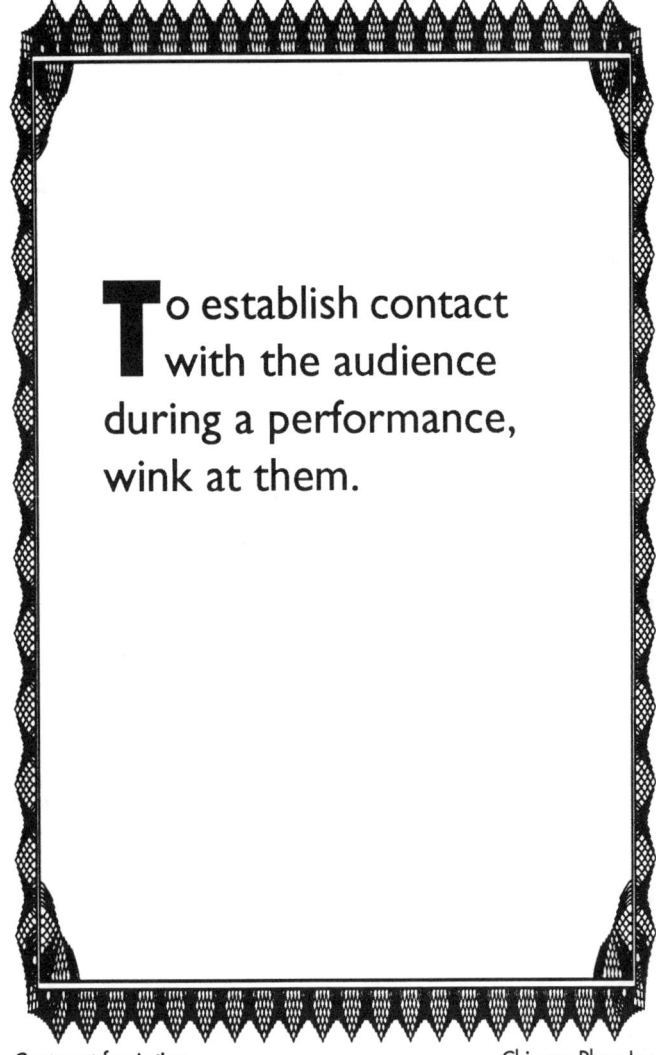

To establish contact with the audience during a performance, wink at them.

Contempt for Acting   Chicago Plays Inc.

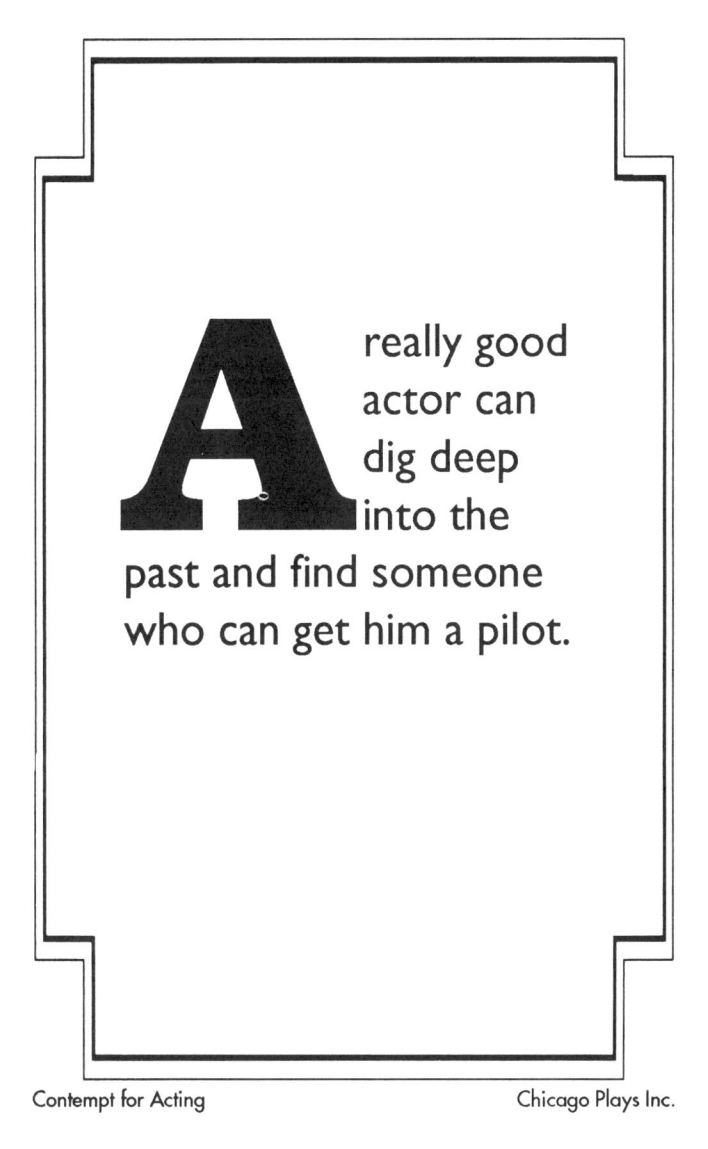

A really good actor can dig deep into the past and find someone who can get him a pilot.

Contempt for Acting — Chicago Plays Inc.

Create close bonds within your cast by seeing who can have the most negative attitude.

Contempt for Acting

Chicago Plays Inc.

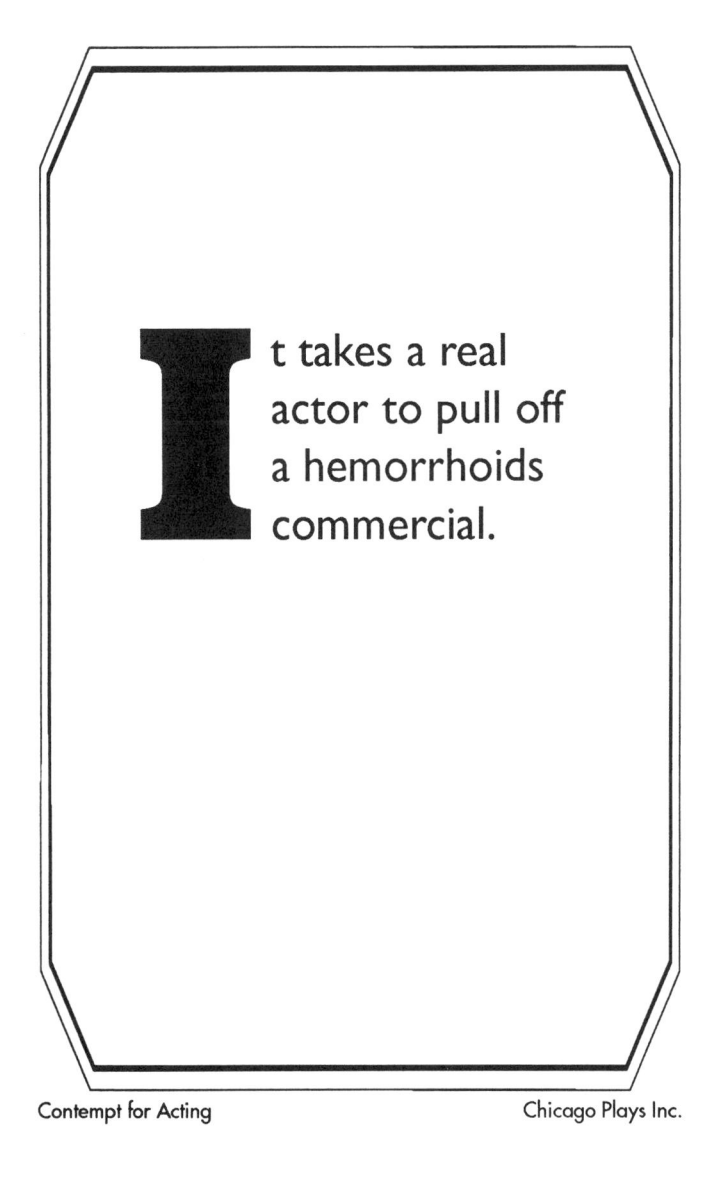

It takes a real actor to pull off a hemorrhoids commercial.

Contempt for Acting   Chicago Plays Inc.

Remember: You're only as good as your agent/director/acting coach says you are.

Contempt for Acting — Chicago Plays Inc.

Every actor is a misunderstood genius. So have fun playing mind games with them.

Why be an actor when you can be a Personality?

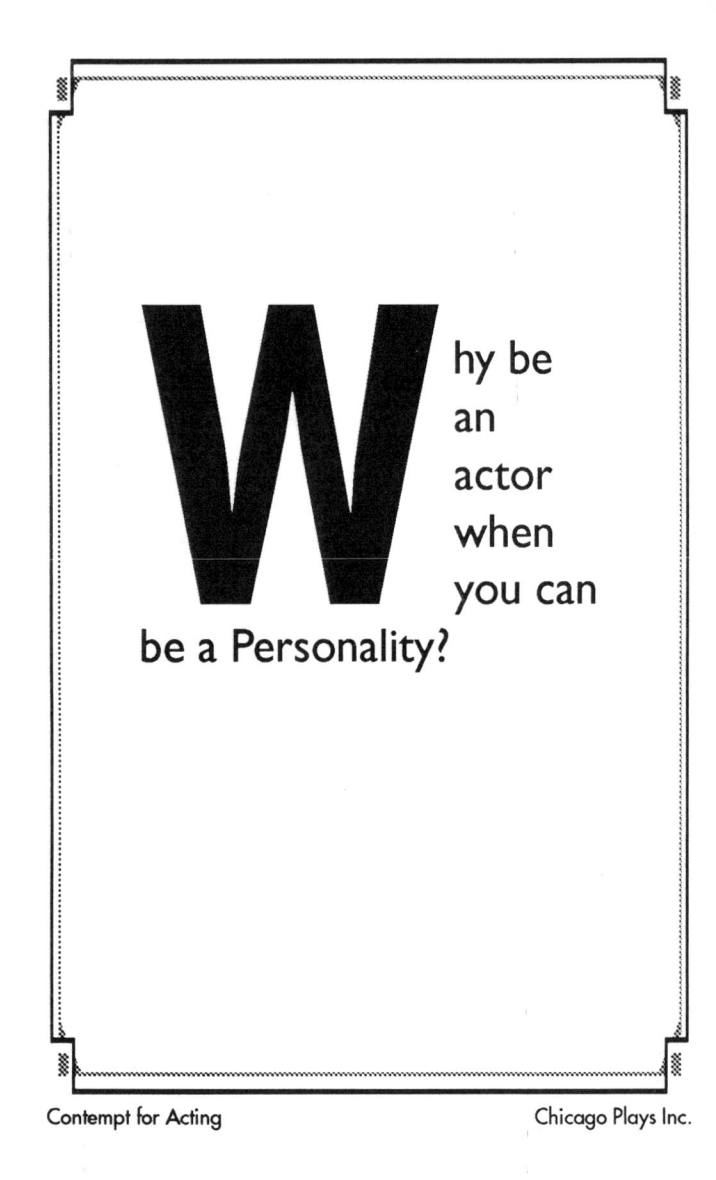

Contempt for Acting   Chicago Plays Inc.

Even more important than a good acting teacher is a good hair stylist.

Contempt for Acting — Chicago Plays Inc.

Use theatre as nothing more than a stepping stone to Fame and Fortune.

Contempt for Acting — Chicago Plays Inc.

Only let the most famous people you know be your friends.

Contempt for Acting · Chicago Plays Inc.

Why limit yourself to just being an actor when you could also be a spokesperson?

Contempt for Acting   Chicago Plays Inc.

What good are all these acting lessons if you're too ugly to be on **Baywatch**?

Contempt for Acting — Chicago Plays Inc.

Fame is knowing how to properly exploit yourself.

Contempt for Acting   Chicago Plays Inc.

If your character needs a motivation, try "to get laid."

Contempt for Acting — Chicago Plays Inc.

The best source for monologues is 976-LICK.

Contempt for Acting

Chicago Plays Inc.

If someone asks you to do a monologue, tell him to do one first.

Contempt for Acting — Chicago Plays Inc.

Any book can tell you how to act, so buy the cheapest.

Contempt for Acting   Chicago Plays Inc.

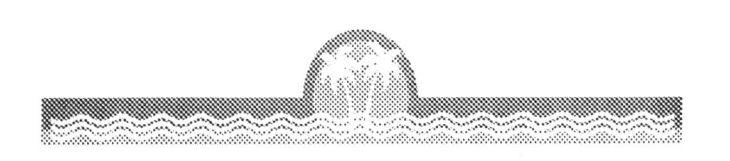

𝔘se your resume as a forum for your political beliefs.

Contempt for Acting — Chicago Plays Inc.

Use auditions as an opportunity to learn about other actors' religious beliefs.

Contempt for Acting — Chicago Plays Inc.

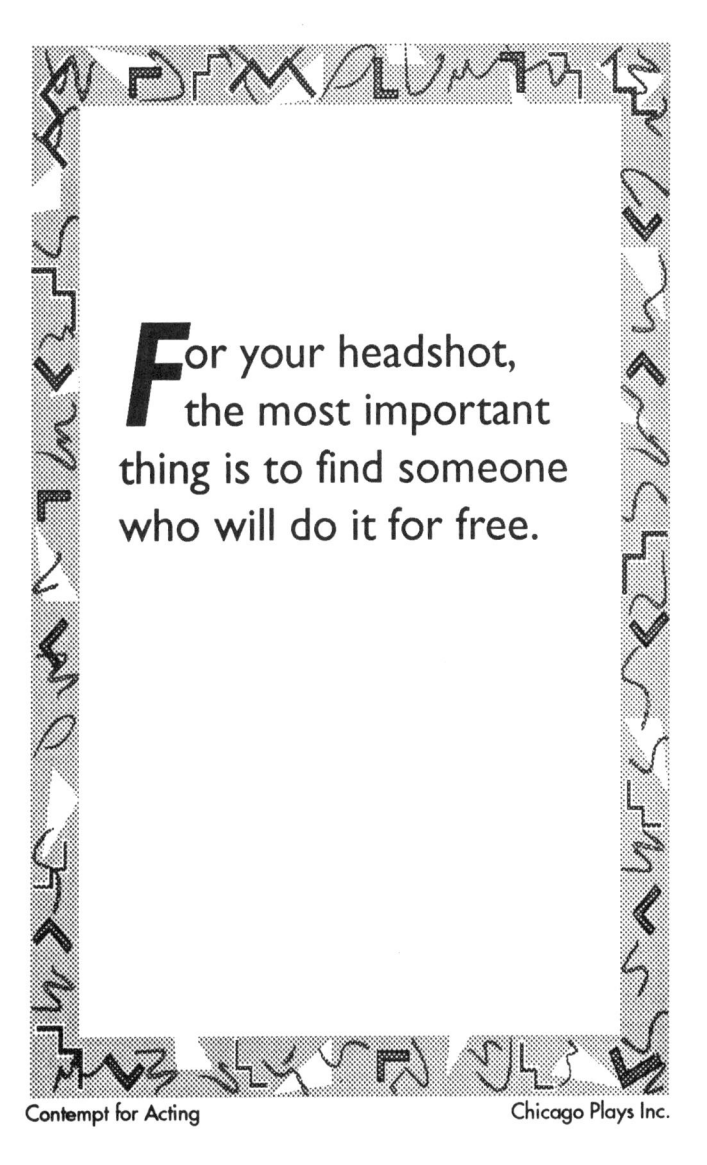

*F*or your headshot, the most important thing is to find someone who will do it for free.

Contempt for Acting — Chicago Plays Inc.

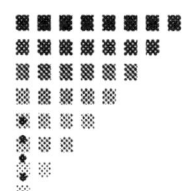

To show your sensitive side, have your headshot taken while holding a teddy bear.

Contempt for Acting

Chicago Plays Inc.

When auditioning, address the director as "Your Gorgeousness."

Contempt for Acting   Chicago Plays Inc.

Crank call agents.

Contempt for Acting   Chicago Plays Inc.

Establish your importance by always being late.

Contempt for Acting · Chicago Plays Inc.

*P*ay for your success in cold hard cash.

Contempt for Acting   Chicago Plays Inc.

If directors have a nickname for you, they'll never forget who you are. Try being known as "The Whiner," "The Flirt," "Queen Evil," "Desperately Seeking Prozac" or "The Guy with a Telephone Pole Up his Butt."

Establish close bonds with fellow actors by saying, "I'd say you were self-absorbed, but your head's so far up your ass you wouldn't hear."

Contempt for Acting　　　　　　　　Chicago Plays Inc.

If the role is between you and one other person, whisper, "If I don't get this part, I'm going to kill your parents."

Contempt for Acting — Chicago Plays Inc.

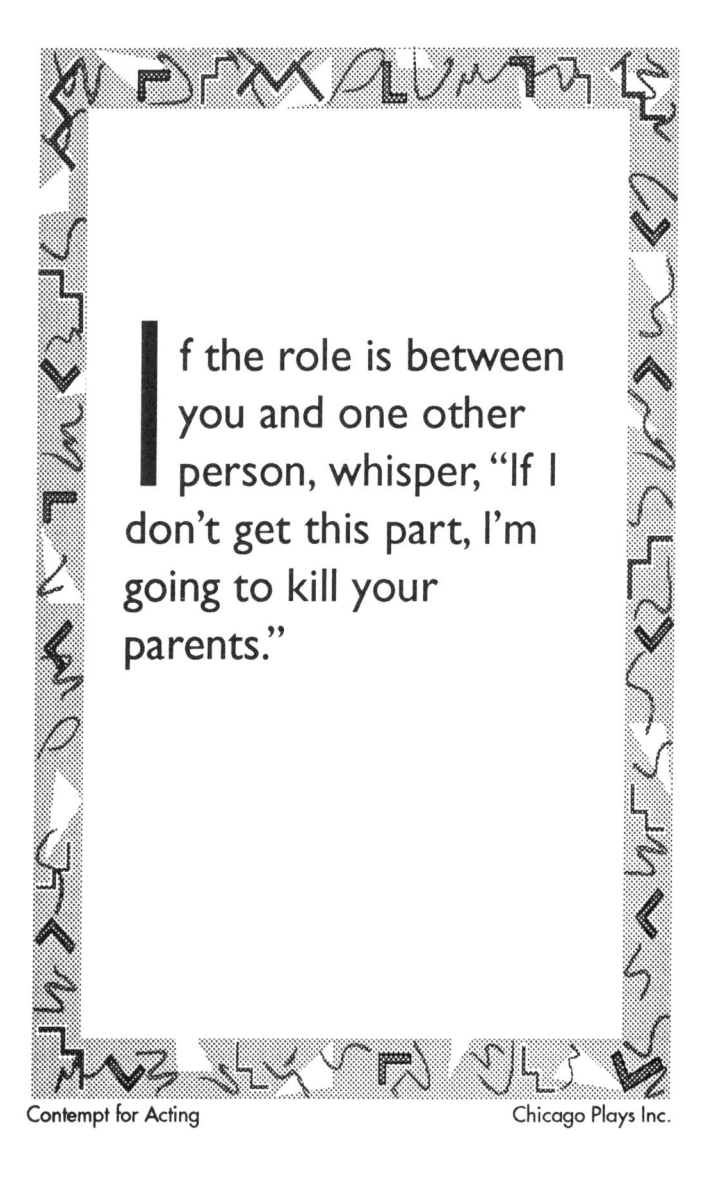

When you're finished with an audition, don't forget to remind the director, "I know where you live."

Contempt for Acting — Chicago Plays Inc.

Three important things to remember for an audition:
1. No matter what kind of part you're reading for, bring in a riding crop and swat yourself occasionally.
2. If the other actor is making you look stupid, spit on him.
3. When you're done, tear the copy to shreds so no one else can use it.

Contempt for Acting — Chicago Plays Inc.

Go to press nights and sneak onstage, pretending to be a character from the play.

Contempt for Acting　　　　　　　　　　　Chicago Plays Inc.

Take bribes from understudies and fake sick.

Contempt for Acting · Chicago Plays Inc.

Play the part exactly like the movie.

Contempt for Acting   Chicago Plays Inc.

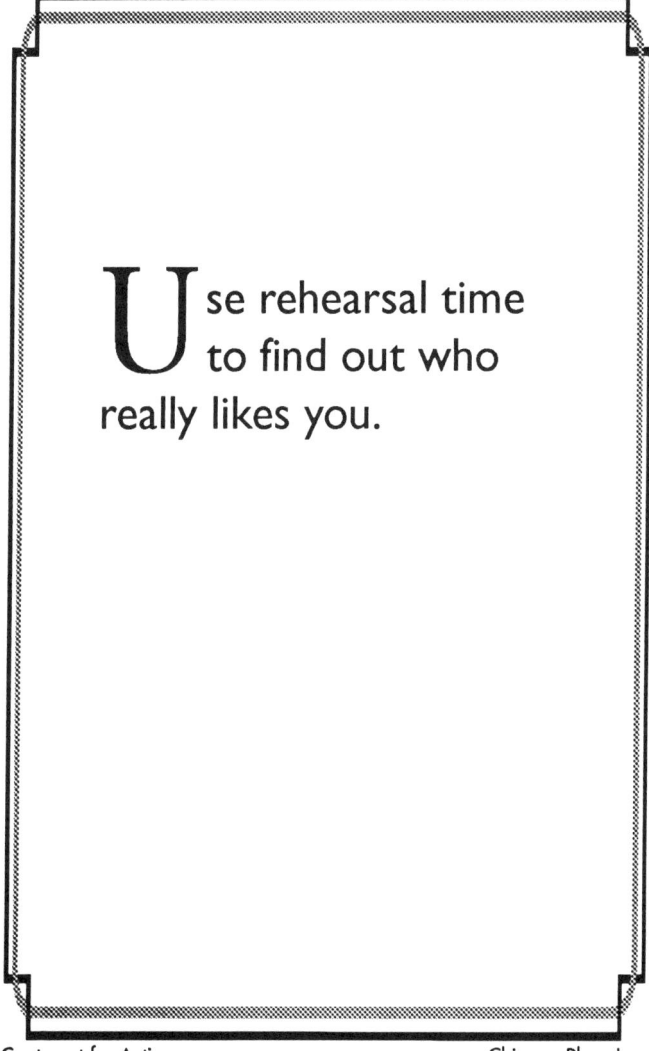

Use rehearsal time to find out who really likes you.

Break into casting offices and steal headshots of anyone who might be your type.

Contempt for Acting — Chicago Plays Inc.

If cast as an extra for a film, trip and fall on every take.

Contempt for Acting Chicago Plays Inc.

When someone else is reading for your part, send them invisible hate bombs and make choking noises.

Contempt for Acting   Chicago Plays Inc.

Spot directors at parties, grab their legs and refuse to let go until they promise to cast you.

Use a mantra to channel your energies in a single focused direction. Try "I am the box office heavyweight champion of the world."

Contempt for Acting   Chicago Plays Inc.

Stars are made by those who most effectively use socialized sex roles to their advantage.

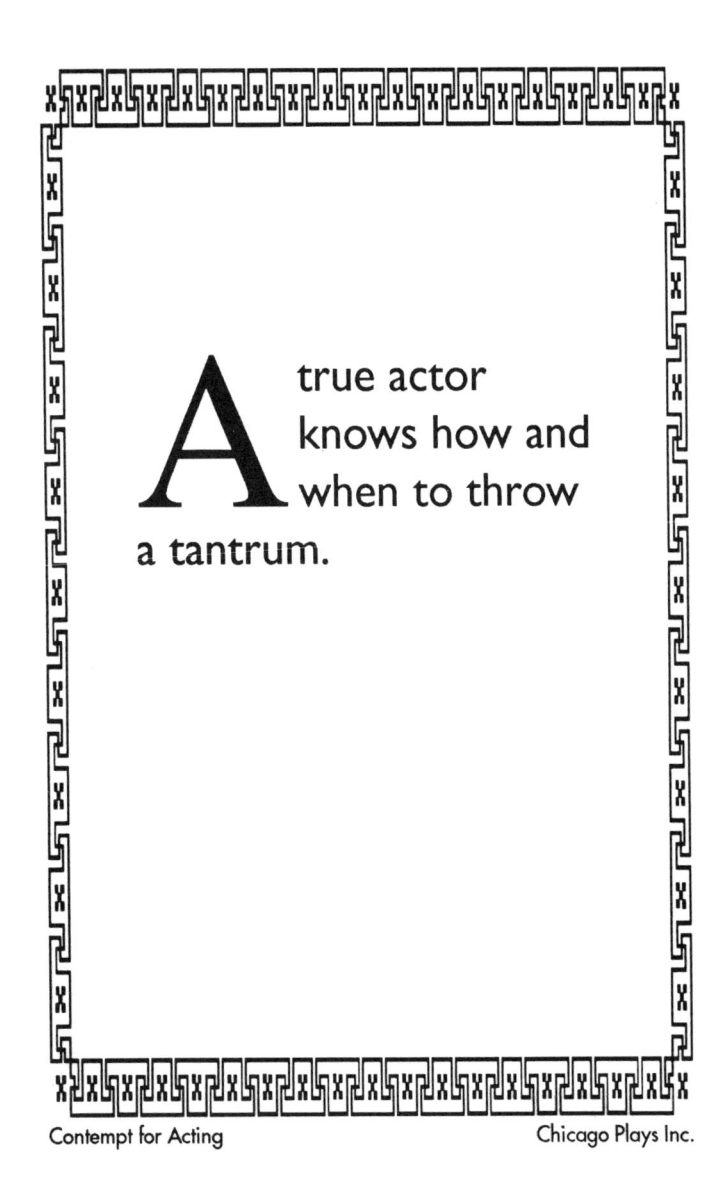

A true actor knows how and when to throw a tantrum.

Contempt for Acting   Chicago Plays Inc.

True genius is knowing how to avoid working and still be famous.

Contempt for Acting — Chicago Plays Inc.

Always keep the fans groveling at your feet.

Contempt for Acting — Chicago Plays Inc.

The amount of your talent is in direct proportion to the size of your entourage.

Contempt for Acting

Chicago Plays Inc.

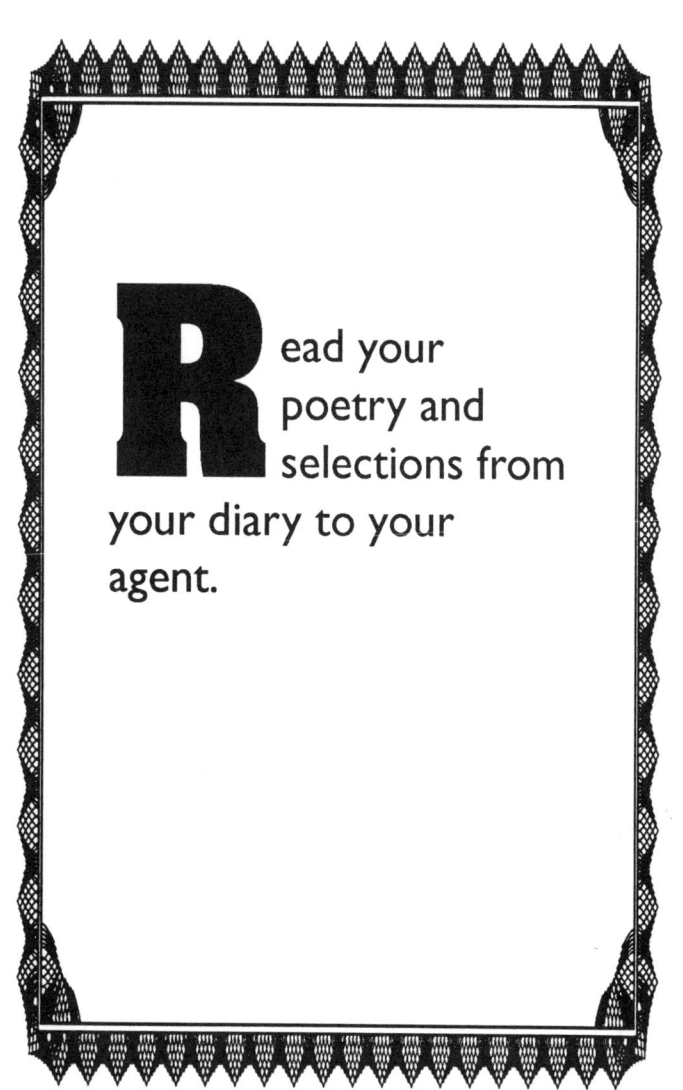

Read your poetry and selections from your diary to your agent.

Contempt for Acting — Chicago Plays Inc.

No matter how wonderful that new class is, always cling to stale habits.

Contempt for Acting — Chicago Plays Inc.

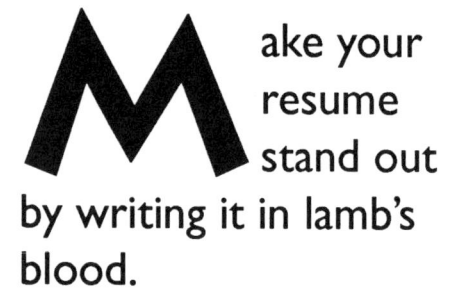

Make your resume stand out by writing it in lamb's blood.

Contempt for Acting — Chicago Plays Inc.

Send ticking packages to those who don't cast you.

Contempt for Acting · Chicago Plays Inc.

The Three Steps to Becoming a Legend:

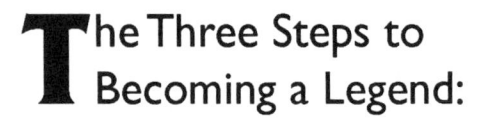

1. Play every part the same way.

2. Cry on Barbara Walters.

3. Make your death memorable.

Contempt for Acting — Chicago Plays Inc.